Motion Imagery Processing and Exploitation (MIPE)

Amado Cordova, Lindsay D. Millard, Lance Menthe, Robert A. Guffey, Carl Rhodes

RAND Project AIR FORCE

The research described in this report was sponsored by the United States Air Force under Contract FA7014-06-C-0001. Further information may be obtained from the Strategic Planning Division, Directorate of Plans, Hq USAF.

Library of Congress Cataloging-in-Publication Data is available for this publication.

ISBN: 978-0-8330-8150-6

The RAND Corporation is a nonprofit institution that helps improve policy and decisionmaking through research and analysis. RAND's publications do not necessarily reflect the opinions of its research clients and sponsors.

Support RAND—make a tax-deductible charitable contribution at www.rand.org/giving/contribute.html

RAND® is a registered trademark.

Preface

The U.S. military has witnessed a dramatic increase in the amount of intelligence data that is collected around the world. Every day, massive amounts of data arrive at military intelligence centers in the form of images collected from earth-orbiting satellites, electronic signals captured by highly specialized equipment, full-motion video (FMV) taken by cameras on board remotely piloted aircraft (RPA) or manned airplanes, and many other means. Making sense of all these data is increasingly challenging, and military analysts risk becoming overwhelmed. As (Ret.) Air Force Lt. Gen. David A. Deptula stated, "We are going to find ourselves in the not too distant future swimming in sensors and drowning in data."[1]

This report defines and investigates the potential of a class of systems, technologies, and capabilities that could alleviate the burden on personnel analyzing motion imagery. We call this class of systems, technologies, and capabilities *motion imagery processing and exploitation* (MIPE).[2]

Findings and recommendations from this report are relevant to organizations that conduct motion imagery intelligence analysis, which include the Air Force, the Army, the Navy, the Marines, and members of the national intelligence community, such as the National Geospatial-Intelligence Agency (NGA). This report should also be of interest to commercial and civil organizations that deal with the challenges of analyzing motion imagery.

This is the last of a series of four RAND reports concerning work sponsored by the Deputy Chief of Staff for Intelligence, Surveillance and Reconnaissance (ISR), Headquarters United States Air Force (HQ USAF); the Assistant Deputy Chief of Staff for ISR, HQ USAF; the Director of Intelligence, Headquarters Air Combat Command (HQ ACC); the Director of ISR Capabilities, HQ USAF; and the Technical Advisor for ISR Capabilities and Integration, HQ USAF, as part of a fiscal year 2010 research effort, "Sizing the U.S. Air Force ISR Force to Meet Future Challenges." The study was conducted within the Force Modernization and Employment Program of RAND Project AIR FORCE. The other three reports are as follows:

- Amado Cordova, Lance Menthe, Lindsay D. Millard, Kirsten M. Keller, Carl Rhodes, and Jeffrey Sullivan, *Emerging Technologies for Intelligence Analysts: Recommendations for the Air Force DCGS Enterprise*, Santa Monica, Calif.: RAND Corporation, 2012, not available to the general public.

---

[1] David A. Deptula, keynote speech, C4ISR Journal Conference, Arlington, Va., October 2009. (Ret.) Lt. Gen. Deptula was the first Air Force Deputy Chief of Staff for Intelligence Surveillance and Reconnaissance. That position is currently held by Lieutenant General Robert P. Otto.

[2] We will also define a closely related (but distinct) class of systems, technologies, and capabilities that we call *motion imagery distribution and storage* (MIDS). The focus of this report is MIPE.

- Amado Cordova, Kirsten M. Keller, Lance Menthe, and Carl Rhodes, *Virtual Collaboration for a Distributed Enterprise,* Santa Monica, Calif.: RAND Corporation, RR-153-AF, 2013. As of October 15, 2013:
http://www.rand.org/pubs/research_reports/RR153.html

- Lance Menthe, Amado Cordova, Carl Rhodes, Rachel Costello, and Jeffrey Sullivan, *The Future of Air Force Motion Imagery Exploitation: Lessons from the Commercial World,* Santa Monica, Calif.: RAND Corporation, TR-1133-AF, 2012. As of October 15, 2013:
http://www.rand.org/pubs/technical_reports/TR1133.html

RAND Project AIR FORCE

RAND Project AIR FORCE (PAF), a division of the RAND Corporation, is the U.S. Air Force's federally funded research and development center for studies and analyses. PAF provides the Air Force with independent analyses of policy alternatives affecting the development, employment, combat readiness, and support of current and future aerospace forces. Research is conducted in four programs: Force Modernization and Employment; Manpower, Personnel, and Training; Resource Management; and Strategy and Doctrine.

Additional information about PAF is available on our website:
http://www.rand.org/paf/

Table of Contents

Figures

Summary

Current military operational needs have driven advances in sensor systems and in the airborne platforms that carry them. In particular, they have brought about the rapid development of motion imagery sensors, including both full-motion video (FMV) and wide-area motion imagery (WAMI)[3] sensors. Moreover, advances in telecommunications now allow raw imagery and other raw intelligence to be transmitted to a worldwide distributed set of military intelligence centers. All these technological advances have led to an "information deluge" that threatens to overwhelm military intelligence analysts.

In this report, we focus on a particular class of tools and technologies (motion imagery processing and exploitation [MIPE]) to help military intelligence analysts take better advantage of the information deluge and to enable them to continue to exploit a wide range of motion imagery collections. We define MIPE as the collection of capabilities and enabling technologies, tools, and systems that aid analysts in the detection, identification, and tracking of objects of interest (OOIs), such as humans and vehicles; in the identification of activities of interest (AOIs);[4] and in the characterization of relationships between and among OOIs and AOIs in live and archival video. We focus on motion imagery collections not only because they are growing so rapidly but also because motion imagery is still a relatively new intelligence, surveillance, and reconnaissance (ISR) capability. As the military services move toward more multi-intelligence (multi-INT)[5] work, it is important to bring new capabilities up to par with the old ones.

Observations and Recommendations

PAF examined the needs of motion imagery analysts, identified MIPE capabilities that could assist in meeting those needs, and assessed the technical readiness of MIPE systems. Major observations and recommendations are as follows.

Use MIPE Systems to Focus Analysts' Attention

MIPE systems have the potential to greatly alleviate the burden on analysts who follow the current practice of continuously monitoring a video stream in search of OOIs and AOIs. However, the current state of the art is such that MIPE systems cannot completely replace all

---

[3] The previously used term was *wide-area airborne surveillance* (WAAS). It is being replaced by WAMI. We will use the term *WAMI* throughout this document.

[4] The acronym AOI used in this report for *activity of interest* is not to be confused with *area of interest*.

[5] *Multi-INT* refers to activities that combine multiple intelligence domains (INTs), such as imagery intelligence (IMINT), FMV, and signals intelligence (SIGINT). In this report we consider FMV an intelligence domain separate from IMINT and reserve the latter term for still-imagery intelligence.

human analysts who search for OOIs or AOIs in arbitrary situations.[6] Thus, our first recommendation to military intelligence organizations is to *adopt a "focus-of-attention" concept of operations (CONOP) and to invest in the associated enabling MIPE technologies and systems.* A focus of attention is a cue from a MIPE system that directs the human operator to examine a particular video frame or subframe in search of an OOI or AOI. This CONOP and associated MIPE system can greatly reduce the amount of archived video footage that an analyst has to sift through in search of an OOI or AOI. We believe that state-of-the-art MIPE systems can achieve the performance levels required for this application.[7] This CONOP may be also leveraged to effectively exploit WAMI data by automatically directing the analyst to examine a smaller part of the wide-area video footage when an OOI or AOI is detected.[8]

Focus on Specific Target Sets and Environments

Our second recommendation concerning MIPE hinges on the recognition that current state-of-the-art MIPE systems tend to operate well only in restricted environments and with restricted target sets. We recommend that military intelligence organizations *identify which target sets and environments are of most interest to them and direct near-term acquisition toward systems that enable those niche MIPE applications.*[9]

Take Advantage of Multi-INT Tools

Our third recommendation is for military intelligence organizations to *invest in systems that take advantage of many sources of information (e.g., a multi-INT tool)* to augment or supplement the capabilities of the not-as-mature MIPE systems. A multi-INT tool, for example, can leverage the capabilities of a mature intelligence discipline (such as SIGINT) to improve a MIPE system's performance in identifying OOIs and AOIs or in reducing false alarms.

Standardize MIPE Test Plans

To be useful to military operations, MIPE systems must be evaluated under conditions that mimic the real world, utilizing a "truthed" data set—that is, a video stream containing real

---

[6] Consequently, the results from MIPE analysis are heavily dependent on human interpretation.

[7] That is, high confidence in not missing the OOI or AOI (low probability of false negatives) can be achieved, but not necessarily high confidence in not misidentifying another object or action for the OOI or AOI of interest (false positives or false alarms). False positives can be better tolerated than false negatives in these applications since they result in analysts wasting time rather than important OOIs or AOIs being missed. We note, however, that false positives take the analyst's attention away from the true positives, and this wasted time may be of importance in certain applications.

[8] However, because of the time sensitivity of current operations, automatic analysis of WAMI footage in near-real time requires a very stringent requirement on not missing OOIs and AOIs (very low probability of false negatives), which may be beyond the current state of the art.

[9] Niche applications should have enough operational utility—for example, enough targets of interest—to justify the investment.

targets whose identity, location, and number are known at all times. Thus, our next recommendation is for military intelligence organizations to *standardize their MIPE test plans.* Metrics for testing these systems should be developed and standardized; in this report, we have suggested several metrics. The test plan should make use of truthed data sets to evaluate the capabilities of candidate technologies and systems.

Take Advantage of Near-Term MIPE Capabilities, Such as Background Subtraction

Our last recommendation concerning MIPE is that, *in the near term, military intelligence organizations employ MIPE systems based on "low-hanging fruit" technologies,*[10] *such as those systems that perform background subtraction.* A background subtraction algorithm could automatically indicate whether the foreground of a video feed has changed significantly between frames, thus directing an analyst to return his or her attention to the changing scene. Conversely, if the scene is not changing significantly, the analyst may be free to attend to other tasks. These systems may also assist an analyst in exploring a relatively unpopulated region using a WAMI sensor. The background subtraction algorithm may then direct him or her to focus on areas of the WAMI feed in which there is some activity.

---

[10] By "low-hanging fruit," we mean technologies that are already mature and are relatively easy to implement.

Acknowledgments

The authors want to thank our sponsors for their thoughtful guidance throughout this project. We are grateful for their assistance.

We are also deeply appreciative of the many Air Force officers, airmen, and civilian personnel who shared their time and expertise with us. These include personnel from the 480th ISR Wing, the 497th ISR Group, the 548th ISR Group, the 11th Intelligence Squadron (IS), the 31st IS, and the Air Force ISR Agency and many others who patiently helped us over the course of numerous discussions and visits.

Many thanks also are due to our colleagues Col Rich Moorhead, Col David J. Gibson, Scott C. Hardiman, Larry Hanser, Matthew E. Boyer, and Abbie Tingstad for their advice and assistance on many aspects of this project.

Finally, we are also thankful to those who reviewed an earlier draft of this document:[11] Douglas Meyer and Steven Dello Russo from ACC/A2; Linda Nichols from ACC; Mark Mankowski from ACC; two directors of operations (DO-1 and DOK) from the 480th Intelligence, Surveillance and Reconnaissance Wing (ISRW); the 480th ISW/XCT; Elliot Axelband from RAND; and Nancy Cooke from Arizona State University and science director of the Cognitive Engineering Research Institute in Mesa, Ariz.

The generosity of all of these experts made this work possible.

---

[11] Amado Cordova, Lance Menthe, Lindsay D. Millard, Kirsten M. Keller, Carl Rhodes, and Jeffrey Sullivan, *Emerging Technologies for Intelligence Analysts: Recommendations for the Air Force DCGS Enterprise*, Santa Monica, Calif.: RAND Corporation, 2012, not available to the general public.

Abbreviations

ACC   Air Combat Command

AF   Air Force

AFB   Air Force Base

AFISRA   Air Force Intelligence, Surveillance and Reconnaissance Agency

AFMC   Air Force Materiel Command

AFRL   Air Force Research Laboratory

AOI   activity of interest

AOR   area of responsibility

ARGUS-IS   Autonomous Real-Time Ground Ubiquitous Surveillance Imaging System

ATC   automated target cueing

ATR   automatic target recognition; assisted target recognition

CAP   Combat Air Patrol

CARS   Contingency Airborne Reconnaissance System

CBVR   content-based video retrieval

CID   confirmatory identification

COMPASE   Comprehensive Performance Assessment of Sensor Exploitation

CONOP   concept of operations

CONUS   continental United States

CVPR   computer vision and pattern recognition

DARPA   Defense Advanced Research Projects Agency

DoD	Department of Defense
EO	electro-optical
ESC	Electronic Systems Command
FAME	Full Motion Video Asset Management Engine
FMV	full-motion video
FOV	field of view
FY	fiscal year
GA	geospatial-intelligence analyst
GEOINT	geospatial intelligence
GRE	geospatial-intelligence reports editor
HAF	Headquarters Air Force
HART	Heterogeneous Airborne Reconnaissance Team
HD	high definition
HQ ACC	Headquarters Air Combat Command
HQ USAF	Headquarters United States Air Force
HUMINT	human intelligence
HVI	high-value individual
IA	imagery analyst
IC	Intelligence Community
ICCSIT	International Conference on Computer Science and Information Technology
IMINT	imagery intelligence
IMS	imagery mission supervisor
INT	intelligence domain

IR	infrared
IRE	imagery report editor
IS	Intelligence Squadron
ISE	imagery support element
ISR	intelligence, surveillance, and reconnaissance
ISREC	intelligence, surveillance, and reconnaissance exploitation cell
I&W	indications and warnings
LOS	line of sight
MAAS	Multimedia Analysis and Archive System
MI	motion imagery
MI-ATR	motion imagery automatic and assisted target recognition
MIDS	motion imagery distribution and storage
MIPE	motion imagery processing and exploitation
MISB	Motion Imagery Standards Board
multi-INT	multi-intelligence
NGA	National Geospatial-Intelligence Agency
NOVA	National System for Geospatial Intelligence Objective Video Architecture
NSG	National System for Geospatial Intelligence
NVS	National System for Geospatial Intelligence Video Services
OEF	Operation Enduring Freedom
OEF-A	Operation Enduring Freedom—Afghanistan
OIF	Operation Iraqi Freedom
OLIVE	online interactive virtual environment

OND	Operation New Dawn
OOI	object of interest
OSD	Office of the Secretary of Defense
PAF	Project AIR FORCE
PCA	principal component analysis
PNNL	Pacific Northwest National Laboratories
POG	practical operating guidelines
QDR	Quadrennial Defense Review
QRC	quick reaction capabilities
ROC	receiver operating characteristic
RPA	remotely piloted aircraft
SAIC	Science Applications International Corporation
SIGINT	signals intelligence
TIR	thermal infrared
TRA	technology readiness assessment
TRD	technical requirements document
TRL	technology readiness level
UAS	unmanned aerial system
UAV	unmanned aerial vehicle
USAF	United States Air Force
VIRAT	Video and Image Retrieval and Analysis Tool
VIVID	Video Verification of Identity
VoIP	voice over Internet protocol

VPC   video processing capability

WAAS   wide-area airborne surveillance

WAMI   wide-area motion imagery

Chapter One: Introduction

The "Information Deluge"

In the early 21st century, all sectors of society—from private businesses to governments, scientific and artistic institutions, and individuals—are experiencing a growing flood of information. The giant retailer chain Wal-Mart processes more than one million customer transactions per hour, feeding databases estimated at 2,500 terabytes,[12] which is the equivalent of 167 times the information in the U.S. Library of Congress.[13] The telescope used for the Sloan Digital Sky Survey collected more data in its first few weeks of operation during the year 2000 than had been collected in the entire history of astronomy, and its archive has now swelled to 140 terabytes; its successor, the Large Synoptic Survey Telescope, will be able to acquire the same amount of data in only five days.[14] A 2008 study by the International Data Corporation projected that about 1,200 exabytes[15] of digital data would be generated worldwide in the year 2010,[16] and, according to Cisco, by 2013 the amount of traffic flowing over the Internet annually will reach 667 exabytes.[17]

Technological advances have fueled an exponential growth in the rate of digital data generation. These advances are typically represented by the computer industry's Moore's Law, which states that microchips' processing power and storage capacity double approximately every 18 months. Another example of the accelerated rate of data generation is in the new field of genomics: The rate of DNA sequencing is now doubling every nine months.[18] The author of a recent article on genomics describes how his field is outpacing others: "Output from next-generation sequencing has grown from 10 Mb per day to 40 Gb per day on a single sequencer. . . . Such a growth in raw output has outstripped the Moore's Law advances in information technology and storage capacity, in which a standard analysis requires 1 to 2 days on a computer cluster and several weeks on a typical workstation."[19]

The digital data revolution has brought enormous benefits to virtually every sector of society, but it also raises new problems. First, storage capacity is struggling to cope with the deluge of

---

[12] One terabyte is 1,000,000,000,000 bytes.

[13] "Data, Data Everywhere," *The Economist*, February 25, 2010.

[14] "Data, Data Everywhere," T2010.

[15] One exabyte is one million terabytes, or 1,000,000,000,000,000,000 bytes.

[16] "All Too Much: Monstrous Amounts of Data," *The Economist*, February 25, 2010.

[17] "Data, Data Everywhere," 2010.

[18] Scott D. Kahn, "On the Future of Genomic Data," *Science*, Vol. 331, February 2011, p. 11.

[19] Kahn, 2011.

data. Second, it is challenging to ensure data security and to protect privacy when information is widely shared via the Internet. Third (and most importantly for this report), it is becoming increasingly difficult to "make sense" of the data, or, as Google's chief economist explains, "data are widely available; what is scarce is the ability to extract wisdom from them."[20]

The Information Deluge in Military Intelligence

The U.S. military has not been immune from the effects of the information deluge. Advances in telecommunications allow immediate transmission of information collected by sensors in theater to military intelligence centers around the world. Every day, massive amounts of data arrive at these intelligence centers in the form of images collected from earth-orbiting satellites, electronic signals captured by highly specialized equipment, full motion video (FMV) taken by cameras on board remotely piloted aircraft (RPA) or manned airplanes, and many other means. Making sense of all these data is increasingly challenging: military analysts risk becoming overwhelmed. As (Ret.) Air Force Lt. Gen. David A. Deptula stated, "We are going to find ourselves in the not too distant future swimming in sensors and drowning in data."[21]

The motion imagery information deluge that military intelligence organizations are currently facing was the result of technological advances in the areas of information collection means (particularly sensors)[22] and in telecommunications.

Advances in Motion Imagery Sensors, Telecommunications, and Platforms

Motion imagery data, in particular, has presented both an opportunity and a challenge for intelligence analysts. Over the past decade, the need to accurately locate and identify elusive targets during irregular warfare and counterinsurgency operations drove the demand for a wide array of sophisticated ISR systems and sensor technologies. One of the new ISR capabilities that became very popular among commanders in Iraq and Afghanistan was motion imagery, which is defined as "any imaging system that collects at a rate of one frame per second (1 Hz) or faster, over a common field of regard."[23] Full-motion video (FMV) is a subset of motion imagery that is transmitted at television-like frame rates (that is, 24 to 60 Hz). 24 Hz is the minimum frame rate at which video appears fluid to the eye.[24] FMV sensors are typically carried by RPAs and by some manned airplanes. Ground commanders at all levels request RPAs equipped with FMV sensors to provide overhead surveillance and advance warning of danger to convoys and to any

---

[20] "Data, Data Everywhere," 2010.

[21] David A. Deptula, keynote speech, C4ISR Journal Conference, Arlington, Va., October 2009.

[22] Not every information collection means is a sensor. For example, human intelligence (HUMINT) pertains to information collection means that could be hardly called sensors.

[23] Department of Defense/Intelligence Community/National System for Geospatial Intelligence (DoD/IC/NSG) Motion Imagery Standards Board (MISB), *Motion Imagery Standards Profile Version 5.4*, December 3, 2009.

[24] DoD/IC/NSG MISB, 2009.

patrol mission in which troops may risk being ambushed by insurgents. Reportedly, many commanders are reluctant to plan a convoy mission without such overwatch.[25]

In addition to FMV, the military services are now deploying wide-area motion imagery (WAMI) sensors to theater. WAMI covers a much wider geographic area than FMV, but at a lower frame rate. It permits persistent, high-resolution surveillance at the level of square miles rather than city blocks. This capability represents another milestone in the technological advance of motion imagery collections. Imagery on that scale, available in near–real time to commanders on the ground, represents a significant increase in the capability to assist operational planning and decisionmaking.

The bandwidth requirements to transmit the full image collected by a WAMI sensor are large, but WAMI sensors also provide "chip-outs": video chips that cover delimited subareas and that can be received by ground terminals.[26] In terms of area covered, each WAMI chip-out covers approximately the same ground area as a single soda-straw (FMV feed).[27] The first developmental increment of WAMI was the Gorgon Stare sensor package.[28]

Advances in telecommunications and RPA platforms have further enhanced the utility of FMV and WAMI. Advanced telecommunications networks, including satellite links and associated wireless and fiber-optic networks, have enabled the military to control RPAs from afar, to maintain persistent ISR orbits over areas of interest, and to transmit the motion imagery (and all other data) to geographically separated sites and line-of-sight (LOS) terminals in near–real time. All of these factors greatly increase the amount of data that flows to intelligence analysts. In the Air Force, for example, the motion imagery from medium-altitude ISR platforms has already grown substantially since the beginning of the conflicts in Iraq and Afghanistan. With the addition of new collectors and new sensors—especially the WAMI sensors—the amount of data could increase by orders of magnitude. For example, the Autonomous Real-Time Ground Ubiquitous Surveillance Imaging System (ARGUS-IS), a WAMI system under development, is capable of collecting over 400 GB per second.[29]

Challenges for Intelligence Analysts

The ability to collect information anywhere and at any time has been an enormous benefit to U.S. military operations, but it has not come without a price. To be of value to the warfighter, data collected by ISR platforms typically must be converted into "actionable intelligence"—

---

[25] See, for example, Christopher Drew, "The Military Is Awash in Data from Drones," *New York Times*, January 11, 2010.

[26] Brigadier General VeraLinn Jamieson, untitled entry, *C4ISR Journal*, October 1, 2009.

[27] However, because it transmits motion imagery at only 2 frames per second, a WAMI chip-out is not considered equivalent to FMV.

[28] In this report, we refer to both WAMI and FMV collections as "motion imagery."

[29] William Matthews, "One Sensor To Do The Work of Many: BAE, DARPA Lash Up Hundreds of 5-Megapixel Camera Chips," *Defense News*, March 1, 2010.

namely, information that is relevant to commanders in the field and that is presented in a form that they can use. This intelligence must also be delivered to those who need it in a timely manner. These tasks become more challenging as the speed and volume of information collection increases.

In addition to the information deluge associated with current conflicts, military intelligence organizations will face other major challenges in the 21st century. Many of these challenges will require analysis of motion imagery. Intelligence organizations need to be prepared to provide support for a wide range of possible operations, including major combat operations, the global fight against terrorist organizations, and peacekeeping and humanitarian relief missions around the world.

Motion Imagery Processing and Exploitation

This report discusses a set of technology enablers, which we call *motion imagery processing and exploitation* (MIPE), that can help military intelligence organizations more effectively manage and analyze the deluge of motion imagery in current and future conflicts. We define MIPE as the class of technologies, systems, and capabilities that have these purposes:

- to aid in the detection, identification, and tracking of humans, vehicles, and other objects of interest (OOIs) in live and archival video, with or without associated metadata[30]
- to aid in the identification of human actions and activities of interest (AOIs) in live and archival video
- to aid in the characterization of relationships between and among OOIs and AOIs
- to facilitate any subsequent analysis, such as multi-intelligence (multi-INT) fusion, network analysis, and data visualization.

Together, the above will be referred to as *MIPE functions*. The technical capabilities to perform these functions in an automated fashion, or to assist analysts in performing these functions, will be referred to as *MIPE capabilities*. Similarly, a MIPE system is any tool designed to provide one or more MIPE capabilities.[31]

Before proceeding with a thorough discussion on MIPE, we want to make the distinction between MIPE and a closely related class of capabilities that we call motion imagery distribution and storage (MIDS). MIDS refers to the systems, technologies, and capabilities that aid the analyst in archival storage, archival search, live search,[32] delivery, and collaboration. Simply put,

---

[30] Metadata is text or audio that is attached to an image or video to facilitate data mining.

[31] Note that tools that cannot perform MIPE functions per se can still provide MIPE capabilities. For example, a tool that would help an analyst identify an AOI within motion imagery would provide a MIPE capability, but it would still be the analyst who actually performs the MIPE function of identification. Tools that assist analysts in performing MIPE functions are an important class of MIPE systems, which we describe later in this report.

[32] Note that search in the MIDS context means only to browse an index or query a database of motion imagery; it does not refer to the more-challenging MIPE function that involves analyzing the motion imagery itself, such as finding a specific vehicle within an image or image sequence. The MIPE function is explained later in the report.

the purpose of a MIDS system is to make all relevant motion imagery intelligence products available to users on request. At present, military motion imagery is distributed and stored in different ways, varying with theater and collector, and the databases are often not linked. Military MIDS systems will benefit from new commercial tools and technologies that allow more-sophisticated methods of managing and retrieving motion imagery. Examples are TiVo and YouTube, which deliver streaming video on demand,[33] and Google, Netflix, and iTunes, which can tailor complex search results to specific users based on user-added tags and previous searches.[34]

MIDS and MIPE intersect to some extent, and the same system may provide both MIDS and MIPE capabilities. For example, the MIPE functions of OOI and AOI detection and identification may be used to organize the video into a searchable database by generating tags or signatures (metadata). These tags may be used by the MIDS functions of archival search and live search to query the database. Moreover, quality MIPE is dependent on quality MIDS—that is, we cannot successfully perform processing and exploitation using a data set that was made poor by low-fidelity distribution and storage.[35]

In the remainder of this report, our focus will be on MIPE. Although many technologies may provide MIPE capabilities, much of the relevant research and development lies in the field of motion imagery automatic and assisted target recognition (MI-ATR). Historically, the term *automatic target recognition* has been associated with technology that promises to detect and identify targets without the need for human intervention, whereas the term *assisted target recognition* has been associated with technology that aims to help human analysts detect and identify targets via cueing or other methods. However, there is increasing room for interpretation in each, and both can enable MIPE capabilities. For this reason, we use the term MI-ATR broadly in this report to discuss both technologies that have a human in the loop and those that do not.

Organization of This Report

This report summarizes PAF's analysis of how MIPE capabilities may help intelligence analysts handle the information deluge in motion imagery. We examined the needs of motion imagery analysts, identified MIPE capabilities that could assist in meeting those needs, and assessed the technical readiness of MIPE systems. The report is organized as follows. In Chapter

---

[33] Streaming video on demand is motion imagery that can be "pulled" by the user when desired and that commences playback almost immediately. Because the user can view the imagery without having the entire file (or in the case of live broadcast, when there is no such file), streaming video requires specialized video compression techniques.

[34] George Toderici, Hrishikesh Aradhye, Marius Pasca, Luciano Sbaiz, and Jay Yagnik, "Finding Meaning on YouTube: Tag Recommendation and Category Discovery," in *2010 IEEE Conference on Computer Vision and Pattern Recognition (CVPR)*, June 13–18, 2010, pp. 3447–3454.

[35] As a final comment on MIDS, current MIDS functions in military intelligence organizations tend to be executed by machines, whereas MIPE functions are predominantly performed by human analysts with the help of machines.

Two, we survey the MI-ATR functions, their current level of development, and their potential applications for imagery intelligence analysts in terms of providing MIPE capabilities. Chapter Three describes existing or developing MIPE systems and discusses how the military services may go about testing and selecting the systems that are best suited to their needs. Chapter Four summarizes our observations and recommendations regarding the evaluation, testing, investment, and acquisition of MIPE systems.

Chapter Two: Motion Imagery Automatic and Assisted Target Recognition

As stated in Chapter One, although many technologies provide MIPE capabilities, much of the relevant research and development lies in the field of MI-ATR. MI-ATR has its roots in the field of computer vision, a relatively new field of study encompassing the science and technology that enables machines to extract information from an image or sequence of images.[36] The original goal of computer vision was to develop visual perception techniques to help mimic human intelligence in robots; it was not until the 1970s, when computers became capable of processing moderately large sets of image data, that a more focused study of the field emerged.

Four broadly defined functions within this field apply to MI-ATR: *instance recognition*, which determines whether an image or a sequence of images contains an instance of a specific object; *category recognition*, which determines whether a sequence of images contains an object that fits a general category; *activity recognition*, which determines whether a sequence of images depicts a specific human action or activity; and *tracking*, which follows the movement of objects through a sequence of images.

It is worth noting that all these recognition and tracking functions can be performed more easily by a trained human being, albeit for only one motion imagery stream at a time. Computer vision techniques do not currently allow for automatic recognition of a specific object or action (e.g., a particular individual) in a generic situation (e.g., a busy intersection, a bus stop, a rural setting) with a high degree of accuracy. Furthermore, there is no consensus among researchers as to when this level of performance might be achieved for these functions.

This chapter describes MI-ATR functions, their current level of development, and their potential applications to imagery intelligence analysts as part of a MIPE capability.

Instance Recognition

Instance recognition involves recognizing a known, specific object from different vantage points, against cluttered backgrounds, and with partial occlusions. An important subset of this function is facial recognition—i.e., the identification of a specific person.[37] Object detection is often (but not always) considered a prerequisite for instance recognition. A popular example of

---

[36] In this discussion, data in an "image" is not necessarily measured in the electro-optical bandwidth; it may be hyperspectral, microwave, infrared (IR), etc.

[37] W. Zhao, R. Chellappa, P. J. Phillips, and A. Rosenfeld, "Face Recognition: A Literature Survey," *ACM Computing Surveys*, Vol. 35, No. 4, December 2008, pp. 399–458.

object detection is the face detector algorithm used by Facebook to frame each face in a photograph before a person identifies those faces.[38]

Feature extraction is one of main methods used to recognize objects in motion imagery. Such algorithms aim to reduce the amount of data required to represent an object by extracting only relevant information. For example, a feature extraction algorithm may scan an image to identify features of interest, such as lines, edges, ridges, corners, blobs, or points, while discarding color entirely[39] (see Figure 2.1). Another common method of feature extraction employs *principal component analysis*—i.e., using a low number of dimensions[40] to optimally approximate data in many dimensions. Once features have been extracted, there is a myriad of subsequent methods that may be employed to analyze them.[41]

Figure 2.1. Example of an Edge Extraction Algorithm

An alternative to feature extraction is *segmentation*.[42] This is a method of "smartly" partitioning an image into many regions or segments. The term "smart" refers to the fact that, after segmentation, the pixels within each region should be similar to one another with respect to

---

[38] Richard Szeliski, *Computer Vision: Algorithms and Applications*, New York: Springer, 2010. Another example is the box used in digital cameras for focusing.

[39] Martin D. Levine, "Feature Extraction: A Survey," in *Proceedings of the IEEE*, Vol. 57, No. 8, August 1969.

[40] By *dimensions*, we mean spatial coordinates, spectral components, features, moments of histogram representations, or other entities that can be represented by a vector in a multidimensional space.

[41] Levine, 1969.

[42] Segmentation may be used in conjunction with feature extraction—i.e., first segmenting the photo and then looking for a specific feature within the segments.

some characteristic or computed property, such as color, intensity, or texture. The goal of segmentation is to distinguish objects and identify boundaries in images. Some of the earliest approaches to facial recognition involved attempting to locate distinctive areas of the face, such as the eyes, and then measure the distance between them.[43]

Currently, computer vision methods of instance recognition are at varying levels of maturity. Facial recognition methods are arguably the most mature; the technology is well developed and commercially available. Today's face recognizers work best when they are given full frontal images of faces under relatively uniform illumination conditions. Although computers cannot yet pick out suspects from thousands of people streaming in front of a video camera, their ability to distinguish among a small number of family members and friends is apparent even in consumer-level photo applications, such as Picasa and iPhoto.[44]

More general instance recognition algorithms are less mature but still sophisticated enough to be useful in some commercial applications, such as Photosynth.[45, 46] However, as with facial recognition algorithms, their performance is highly dependent on the environment. Current computer vision systems are capable of recognizing a specific object, such as a human face, or text—but only in a restricted environment.[47] Parameters of these restricted environments vary wildly, depending on the algorithm, system design, and desired performance. Recently (since 2007), research in methods that utilize scene context to aid in instance recognition has proliferated in the field of computer vision; these algorithms promise to significantly improve the performance of instance recognition algorithms.[48, 49]

Given the state of the art, it is unlikely that current airborne ISR platforms and sensors will be able to perform fully automated instance recognition in current operational environments. Performing facial recognition with an RPA, for example, would be extremely challenging with current sensors and with traditional MI-ATR methods. For MI-ATR face recognition methods to work, the camera must be facing the subject (the target), an impossible task when the sensor is

---

[43] Surendra Gupte, Osama Masoud, Robert R. K. Martin, and Nikolaos P. Papanikolopoulos, "Detection and Classification of Vehicles," *IEEE Transactions on Intelligent Transportation Systems*, Vol. 3, No. 1, March 2002.

[44] W. Zhao, R. Chellappa, P. J. Phillips, and A. Rosenfeld, "Face Recognition: A Literature Survey," *ACM Computing Surveys*, Vol. 35, No. 4, December 2008, pp. 399–458.

[45] Photosynth is a program that can stitch together several disparate digital photos of the same object or scene into a single 3-D image (Photosynth home page, undated).

[46] Szeliski, 2010.

[47] One example of this capability is demonstrated in the Video Verification of Identity (VIVID) system, developed by the Air Force Research Laboratory (AFRL) and the Defense Advanced Research Projects Agency (DARPA). With some degree of uncertainty, VIVID algorithms can discern between six specific cars on a roadway. This system is discussed in further detail in Chapter Three.

[48] See Chapter Three for more details on the VIVID system.

[49] Sameer Antani, Rangachar Kasturi, and Ramesh Jain, "A Survey on the Use of Pattern Recognition Methods for Abstraction, Indexing, and Retrieval of Images and Video," *The Journal of Pattern Recognition*, Vol. 35, 2002, pp. 945–965.

carried onboard an airborne platform and the target is on the ground. Facial recognition algorithms often measure the distances between the eyes, eyebrows, nose, and mouth, which are unique to every person and distinguishable via a feature recognition algorithm. These measurements are then compared to a database to determine if there is a match. If the camera is not directly facing the subject or part of the face is occluded, these methods do not work because measurements between the distinguishing features cannot be made. However, current instance recognition algorithms could be useful to imagery analysts by providing a "cue" to focus attention on potential areas of interest. Later in this chapter, we propose a "focus-of-attention" concept of operations (CONOP) that uses current instance recognition and other MI-ATR functions to assist motion imagery analysts in critical tasks.

Category Recognition

Category recognition involves the much more challenging problem of recognizing any occurrence of an object in a general category, such as a certain class of military vehicle. For a military imagery analyst, the fact that this is more challenging than instance recognition may be counterintuitive; it is generally easier for a human being to *classify* than to *identify* a target. However, unlike humans, who can easily categorize based on context or experience, machines require rules that can be difficult to define.[50] Even a simple category, such as *chair*, contains such wide variation in color, shape, and size that no simple combination of these features suffices to define it.

The past decade has seen the emergence of sophisticated machine learning techniques applied to recognition functions.[51, 52] Instead of manually defining a category based on preset rules or templates, a computer vision system may "learn" the category through *statistical reasoning*. For example, a computer may search through images to find similar pixel patterns; the more similar the pattern, the more likely the objects are to be in the same category. A human may be used to provide initial feedback to this process—e.g., by affirming which objects are of the same category—thereby allowing the computer vision system to refine its decision process.

Category recognition remains largely unsolved in computer vision; category recognition algorithms have so far only performed well in a closed world—i.e., in an environment in which the number of possible categories for images is known and small.[53] When this MI-ATR function is better developed, military systems will be able to automatically recognize specific classes of military vehicles or other categories of interest in battlefield motion imagery in real time. In the

---

[50] Antani, Kasturi, and Jain, 2002.

[51] Robin R. Murphy and Brent Taylor, "A Survey of Machine Learning Techniques for Automatic Target Recognition," *IEEE Transactions on Pattern Analysis and Machine Intelligence*, Golden Co.: Department of Mathematical and Computer Sciences, Colorado School of Mines, 2007.

[52] This trend coincides with the increased availability of immense quantities of partially labeled data on the Internet.

[53] Antani, Kasturi, and Jain, 2002.

near term, category recognition may contribute to a focus-of-attention CONOP, as described below.

Activity Recognition and Background Subtraction

Activity recognition is the function that relies most on the "motion" part of motion imagery, as it requires identifying human movements as specific actions (that is, simple motion patterns executed by a single human), as well as activities, which involve more complex motion patterns and may involve the coordinated actions of several humans with specific objects.[54] In general, activity recognition is the most challenging form of recognition, as it involves recognizing both objects and how they interact over time. Human beings have extensive knowledge that they apply to their interpretation of an activity, including cultural norms, specific activities seen on a stretch of road, gait patterns indicating gender, and the presence of children. If machines are to interpret activity as well as humans do, they will need to also draw on this type of knowledge.

Most activity recognition methods involve some form of feature extraction from sequential frames, followed by an attempt to match these feature sequences to a stored template.[55] Dynamical models may be used to determine whether the feature sequence does in fact represent the motion of a single object. Research in the area of *optical flow*, the apparent motion of individual pixels on an image plane, often serves as a good approximation of the true physical motion of a person. The determination of *point trajectories*, or the trajectories of human bodies or joints relative to an image background, is another method used to infer the activity of the person. However, any errors in the initial feature extraction can easily propagate to higher-level analysis,[56] and the same factors that complicate instance recognition—varying vantage points, background clutter, and partial occlusions—also greatly complicate activity recognition.[57]

Several activity recognition methods are under development, and most systems with this function are currently designed and tested on video sequences acquired in constrained conditions. Furthermore, methods capable of recognizing the wide variability in features that are observed within the same category of activity remain elusive. Although researchers have addressed these issues in specific settings, a systematic and general approach has not been demonstrated.

Background subtraction may be considered a rudimentary form of activity recognition. The goal of background subtraction is to effectively distinguish objects in the foreground of a picture,

---

[54] Pavan Turaga, Rama Chellapa, V. S. Subrahmanian, and Octavian Udrea, "Machine Recognition of Human Activities: A Survey," *IEEE Transactions on Circuits and Systems for Video Technology*, Vol. 18, No. 11, November 2008.

[55] Turaga et al., 2008.

[56] For example, if a feature extraction algorithm mistakes an elbow joint for a knee joint, the motion and action of the associated person will also be misidentified.

[57] Turaga et al., 2008.

which are moving, from the more stagnant background of the scene. However, the background image may not be perfectly fixed, as there may be gradual illumination changes, camera oscillations, a changing camera angle, or moving objects (such as tree branches, waves in the ocean, clouds, and so on). There are several methods to enable background subtraction. The simplest is to obtain an estimate of the background by taking the average or median of several previous frames in the video feed. In other words, the background is defined as the chronological average of each pixel's history. Then this background, or average value, is subtracted from the current video frame to enable discrimination of objects that are moving in the foreground.[58] The current performance of background subtraction methods depends on both the nature of the background scene and the method used. Generally, performance is highest when the background is completely static. A completely static background is a situation often encountered in current RPA video feeds because of the relatively sparse environment, although movement of the camera and/or aircraft will have to be accounted for in the algorithm. Some background subtraction methods have been demonstrated to correctly categorize upwards of 90 percent of pixels as either background or foreground, given a static background. However, if the video background is noisy, this percentage drops significantly.[59] Furthermore, background subtraction methods do not work well if a scene contains many slowly moving objects or if the moving objects are fast relative to the frame rate of the video.

Background subtraction methods are employed successfully in several commercial products. For example, automatic closed-circuit television (CCTV) traffic monitors, such as Siemens' Telscan, have become increasingly prevalent in the United Kingdom to monitor traffic volume.[60] Many video conferencing systems employ background subtraction to reduce the data rate of streaming video and reduce latency time. Finally, background subtraction is also often one of the key enablers of video tracking in televised sports events. The technology has been used to detect and track players, as well as volleyballs and soccer balls.[61]

Tracking

Tracking generally involves solving two basic problems: *motion* and *matching*. The *motion problem* involves predicting the approximate area in which a tracked object is expected to be found in the following frame; the *matching problem* involves identifying the tracked object

---

[58] Massimo Piccardi, "Background Subtraction Techniques: A Review," IEEE International Conference on Systems, Man and Cybernetics, 2004.

[59] Y. Benezeth, P. M. Jodoin, B. Emile, H. Laurent, and C. Rosenberger, "Review and Evaluation of Commonly-Implemented Background Subtraction Algorithms," 19th International Conference on Pattern Recognition, 2008.

[60] Siemens, "Telscan," September 24, 2010.

[61] A. Aristidou, P. Pangalos, and H. Aghvami, "Tracking Multiple Sports Players for Mobile Display," IPCV Conference, 2007.

within that designated area. The matching problem is akin to instance recognition, although it does not actually require the object to be identified.[62, 63]

Tracking algorithms were improved in the 1990s through the incorporation of various *pattern recognition methods*.[64] Pattern recognition methods attempt to find underlying structure in raw data and infer information, based on either a priori knowledge or statistical analysis. Often, segmentation or feature extraction is performed before pattern recognition. A wide range of algorithms may be used in pattern recognition.[65] Although the motion problem in object tracking is well solved, the matching problem suffers from the same immaturity as many instance recognition algorithms. A well-known solution to the motion problem is the Kalman filter, an algorithm that may facilitate optimal estimation of the position and velocity of an object.[66] Kalman filters and other simple predictions of search regions have been adopted widely and successfully for video tracking applications. Algorithms to solve matching problems depend substantially on the complexity of the target and environment; these algorithms have wildly varying degrees of performance. Tracking an object with a simple geometry (such as a window) against a constant background is perhaps the simplest tracking problem and can be solved adequately; tracking has so far been applied successfully only to problems with limited targets and environments.[67] Tracking complex targets against diverse backgrounds or in the vicinity of many similar objects is an active area of research.

The Focus-of-Attention CONOP

The above discussion suggests that significant further development is needed before MI-ATR functions can be incorporated into military systems. This is generally true if a high level of accuracy is required (for example, a very low probability of misidentifying a target) and if the military's expectation is to have a fully automated system. Moreover, there is debate about the utility of systems that promise to fully automate MI-ATR functions—systems that do not include a human in the loop. Until MI-ATR methods can be made adaptable to content, context, and image quality, their utility on the battlefield remains questionable. In the critical task of

---

[62] Here by *identifying* we mean knowing exactly what the OOI is. The computer algorithm still has to know that the OOI is the same one that was previously detected and/or being tracked.

[63] Emanuele Trucco and Konstantinos Plakas, "Video Tracking: A Concise Survey," *IEEE Journal of Oceanic Engineering*, Vol. 31, No. 2, April 2006.

[64] Jan-Olof Eklundh and Henrik I. Christensen, "Computer Vision: Past and Future," in Reinhard Wilhelm, ed., *Informatics: 10 Years Back, 10 Years Ahead (Lecture Notes in Computer Science)*, Springer, 2001, pp. 328–340.

[65] Antani, Kasturi, and Jain, 2002.

[66] A Kalman filter is a computational algorithm that processes measurements to deduce an optimum estimate of the past, present, or future state of a linear system by using a time sequence of measurements of the system behavior, plus a statistical model that characterizes the system and measurement errors, plus initial condition information (Institute for Telecommunications Sciences, "Kalman Filter," August 23, 1996).

[67] Trucco and Plakas, 2006.

identifying the enemy, any fully automated MIPE system with an error rate higher than that of a trained analyst may be unacceptable: In today's order of battle, avoiding both collateral damage and friendly fire is of paramount importance to the warfighter.

We believe that state-of-the-art tools that perform MI-ATR functions can be incorporated into real military MIPE systems today, as long as such functions are *assisting* (instead of replacing) the human analyst. In this regard, we propose a simple, near-term approach (the focus-of-attention CONOP) that can alleviate the burden on motion imagery analysis using existing MIPE capabilities.

The focus-of-attention CONOP consists of the following steps: First, an assisted target recognition MIPE system[68] analyzes video footage without human intervention. Second, the system automatically generates cues based on some preprogrammed criteria. Third, the human operator is directed by these cues to examine the frame or portion of frame that was cued. Finally, the human operator determines whether the frame or subframe contains or is relevant to an OOI or AOI. We emphasize that the final determination is made by a human being and not by the MIPE system.

The focus-of-attention CONOP can also help an analyst to locate potential OOIs and/or AOIs in archived video. In this application, the analyst is interested in a tool that can narrow down his or her search for an OOI or AOI instead of having to sift through hours of video footage.

This CONOP assumes that a relatively large number of false cues (false alarms or false positives) may be acceptable to the analyst. For these applications, false positives can be better tolerated than false negatives because they result in analysts wasting time rather than important OOIs or AOIs being missed.[69] Therefore, we believe that existing MIPE systems can provide the capabilities required to enable this CONOP for this application. Even systems exhibiting false alarm rates that are unacceptable for other applications may be used in this one. Moreover, enabling technologies for this CONOP may be of the assisted target recognition type, which are more mature than those of the automatic target recognition type.

The focus-of-attention CONOP may also aid the human operator in maintaining focus on an OOI across video footage while the frame and vantage point are shifting. For this application, a large number of false alarms may be a drawback, so the human operator may need to be more engaged to make the critical decision on whether the OOI is contained in the cued frame or subframe. This CONOP could also be leveraged to effectively exploit WAMI data. For example, an analyst in charge of exploiting WAMI may not be able to watch the entire wide area with equal attention. Instead of increasing the number of analysts watching the WAMI feed, a focus-

---

[68] This CONOP also works with a fully automated target recognition system, but an assisted target recognition system is sufficient.

[69] However, false positives take the analyst's attention away from the true positives, and this wasted time may be of importance in certain applications.

of-attention CONOP could cue the analyst to a smaller area of the footage when an OOI or AOI is detected.

Conclusion

MI-ATR has made significant progress since the 1970s. Although the MI-ATR functions discussed in this chapter are still in development, the proposed focus-of-attention CONOP can be used at the present time to leverage existing state-of-the-art MIPE systems that make use of those functions to achieve military utility. The next chapter discusses examples of current MIPE systems and how they may be tested and evaluated for use in military intelligence organizations.

Chapter Three: Testing and Evaluating Current and Future MIPE Systems

Examples of MIPE Systems

All of the services and a number of different agencies affiliated with the Department of Defense (DoD) have worked or are working to develop systems that provide MIPE capabilities. However, much of the information on these systems is proprietary and thus not available to the general public. In this chapter, we briefly discuss three representative MIPE systems that use different methods: VIVID, the Video and Image Retrieval and Analysis Tool (VIRAT), and video analytics.[70] We then discuss how military intelligence organizations can go about testing and evaluating current and future systems.

Video Verification of Identity (VIVID)

VIVID is a MIPE system developed by DARPA. Like many such systems under development, VIVID performs the MI-ATR functions of instance recognition and tracking, employing solely MI-ATR methods. The tracking method utilizes feature extraction to solve the matching problem and a Kalman filter to address the motion problem, as described in the previous chapter.[71]

Included in VIVID is a confirmatory identification (CID) module that attempts to recover the location of a vehicle after a loss of track has occurred (perhaps due to dense foliage, high traffic, or other occlusions). The CID module uses feature extraction to build a model of the vehicle and then compares this model to objects in subsequent image frames in an attempt to recognize the vehicle.

Video and Image Retrieval and Analysis Tool (VIRAT)

VIRAT is a MIPE system designed by DARPA to enable search and recognition of actions and activities that occur in overhead aerial video from narrow field-of-view sensors. VIRAT is in development to facilitate assisted target recognition by automatically cueing an analyst to an activity of interest. Furthermore, VIRAT promises to be robust to some variations in

---

[70] As noted earlier, these systems may provide other capabilities as well.

[71] Kyle J. Erickson, Philip M. Hanna, Lori A. Westerkamp, and John C. Mossing, "Evaluation of the VIVID Confirmatory Identification Module," *Automatic Target Recognition XVII, Proceedings of SPIE*, Vol. 6566, 6566B, 2007.

illumination, range, and viewpoint. VIRAT also includes video indexing and retrieval capabilities based on interactive query refinement.[72]

Video Analytics

Video analytics is a system developed at Pacific Northwest National Laboratories (PNNL). Video analytics promises to perform many of the functions traditionally associated with MI-ATR, such as instance recognition (including facial recognition) and tracking.[73]

Video analytics is designed to create a searchable database that can be used to organize large quantities of video without textual or audio metadata tags. Indeed, one of the main advantages of video analytics is that it may not require human operators to generate metadata tags, which can be a resource-demanding and time-intensive task.[74] As part of the system, an algorithm works to identify objects in each image in a video segment based on color and pixel distribution. These objects are then organized, based on similar information content, into a searchable database. Using a substantial, distributed, hybrid multicore processing framework, video content may be ingested, organized, and searched in real time. Video analytics also promises to provide the more advanced MIPE capability of video-based social networking via graph theory.[75, 76]

Additional systems are in various stages of development, and one would expect the number of MIPE systems to grow as the technology matures. Selecting an appropriate system or combination of systems will require thorough testing against well-defined metrics. We discuss an approach to assessment and suggest relevant metrics in the next section.

Evaluating Performance of MIPE Systems

MIPE systems that assist in detection, identification, and tracking of OOIs and AOIs are generally difficult to assess. Determining methods for assessment of these systems is an active area of research by many institutions, including the services, academia, industry, and the intelligence community. As mentioned, the difficulty arises in part because the effectiveness of

---

[72] DARPA Information Processing Techniques Office, "Video and Image Retrieval and Analysis Tool (VIRAT)," November 22, 2010.

[73] On the one hand, video analytics technology has similarities with such traditional MI-ATR methods as feature extraction—it extracts color distribution information in each video frame and target in terms of a 21-component vector—and principal component analysis (PCA)—to reduce the vector to a computable and searchable size. On the other hand, it goes beyond traditional MI-ATR methods by including network analysis, organizational techniques, and video-based social networking via graph theory.

[74] The video analytics technology is explained in more detail in the appendix.

[75] Harold Trease, Robert Farber, Adam Wynne, and Lynne Trease, "High Performance Video Content Analysis Using Hybrid, Multi-Core Processors," in *Proceedings of the 10th IASTED International Conference, Signal and Image Processing*, Kailua-Kona, Hawaii, August 18–20, 2008.

[76] Harold E. Trease and Lynn Trease, "Video Analytics for Indexing, Summarization, and Searching of Video Archives," in *Proceedings of the IASTED International Conference, Signal and Image Processing*, Honolulu, Hawaii, August 17–19, 2009.

this type of MIPE system is highly dependent on the operational environment in which it is utilized.

To be useful to military intelligence operations, MIPE systems must be evaluated under conditions that mimic real-world application of the system, which may include very large target sets and diverse environments. The desired capabilities may also depend on the type of military operation; for example, evaluations of MIPE system performance in irregular warfare may not be relevant to major combat operations. It is also important to note that performance in one area may be heavily dependent on performance in another. For example, the ability of a system to exploit data may depend on previous processing.

AFRL lists 22 conditions that have a high impact on MI-ATR performance,[77] and, as indicated previously, most of the research and development on MIPE capabilities resides in the field of MI-ATR. These conditions include environmental operating conditions (e.g., contrast, illumination, terrain), sensor operation conditions (e.g., resolution, compression, jitter, blur), and target operating conditions (e.g., vehicle type, color, temperature, shadows).

Truthed Data Sets

The expected operating environment is often captured in what is called a "truthed" data set. In this context, a truthed data set is a video stream containing real targets whose identity, location, and number are known at all times. The data set must be produced with specified video parameters under well-defined environmental conditions, and the targets must be geolocated. Developing a truthed data set for military operations is generally difficult and costly, and to repeat the production to simulate a wide range of video parameters and environmental conditions is even more so. Data sets currently available do not fit this definition of a truthed data set. Many data sets contain actual annotated RPA video feed from theater and, therefore, do not satisfy the definition of a truthed data set. Other data sets also have shortcomings. No existing data sets that we are aware of can be used to serve as a validated truthed source.

The AFRL Comprehensive Performance Assessment of Sensor Exploitation (COMPASE) Center has been actively involved in evaluating the CID module of VIVID. As part of the evaluation, a test video stream was used to measure algorithm performance. This test video contains five specific vehicle targets operating in a well-defined environment. AFRL's evaluation showed that the VIVID CID module performed well relative to DARPA milestones in the defined environment. However, the test data set has limited use in quantifying MI-ATR algorithm effectiveness against diverse targets in the current operating environment.[78] Nevertheless, the VIVID data set is a solid first step toward the development of a comprehensive truthed data set—that is, a truthed data set that includes all the relevant target types, as well as all the relevant operating environments.

---

[77] Erickson et al., 2007.

[78] Erickson et al., 2007.

18

Metrics for Evaluating Performance of MIPE Systems

A truthed data set may be used as a standard to measure performance of MIPE systems through such metrics as probability of false alarm and detection rate. Perhaps the most well-known indicator of performance is the receiver operating characteristic (ROC) curve. The ROC curve represents a trade-off between the probability of detecting an object and the probability of false alarm. ROC analysis is appropriate for situations in which each data element indicates either the presence or absence of a signal. For imagery applications, for example, the image contains either no target or exactly one target.[79]

When multiple targets are possible in the same image, a *confuser matrix* is often populated. A confuser matrix shows the probability that any target will be correctly identified, as well as the probability that the target will be incorrectly identified as some other object in the video. With this method, there are a defined number of other objects that the target may be confused with; these are termed *confusers*. For systems that rely on MI-ATR methods, confusers are often chosen based on the expected operating conditions of the specific MI-ATR algorithms.[80]

The metrics to assess MIPE capabilities, however, must go beyond the traditional ROC curve and confuser matrix if they are to assess the capability of a system to characterize relationships between objects and actions or the ability to track an object. These metrics should be applicable to both electro-optical (EO) and IR footage, should apply across the range of environmental conditions, and should be based on the capabilities delivered by the MIPE systems, independent of the methods employed.

Representative metrics for a MIPE system would be

- ability to detect, identify, search for, and track OOIs and AOIs

    - probabilities of detection and identification of specific OOIs and AOIs under varying environmental conditions
    - probability of maintaining track on an OOI with defined obscuration or confusers
    - probability of false alarms

- timeliness

    - time required to detect an OOI or AOI for live video streams (may vary with location of user)
    - estimated change in time required to search the motion imagery database as a function of database size (a measure of algorithm efficiency)

- ease of integration with current architecture

    - required training (in hours) per person or added personnel required
    - cost of software or hardware upgrades to support the MIPE system

---

[79] John M. Irvine, "Assessing Target Search Performance: The Free-Response Operator Characteristic Model," *Optical Engineering*, Vol. 43, No. 12, December 2004.

[80] Lloyd G. Clark, AFRL/RYAA, "AFRL COMPASE Center," PowerPoint presentation, December 17, 2009.

- usability and usefulness when integrated with the human component of the system.

These metrics should evolve over time to represent the changing technology available to systems that perform MIPE capabilities. As an example, the definition of an AOI is likely to become significantly more sophisticated over time, as automated analysis becomes more intelligent and is able to draw on a larger library of knowledge in the same amount of time.

Chapter Four: Conclusions and Recommendations

Systems that provide MIPE capabilities have the potential to revolutionize the way that military intelligence organizations manage and exploit motion imagery collections. Properly tuned to minimize false negatives, a mature MIPE capability could allow an analyst to watch multiple screens at once, with the confidence that the automated system would quickly flag or call out any features that could potentially be of interest. Present practice is to keep "eyes on" only one video at a time to ensure that nothing is missed. Although this is necessary for current operations, a sufficiently proven and effective MIPE system could begin to relieve the analyst of this burden in the future.

This chapter summarizes our major observations and recommendations in the areas of evaluation and testing and investment and acquisition.

Evaluation and Testing

The services are planning limited testing on systems that include MIPE capabilities. However, it is unclear whether these tests include adequate metrics for comparison of a wide range of system performance. The current momentum fueling immediate investment in promising individual technologies is laudable but should be tempered by the understanding that tools capable of providing significant new capabilities must also be assessed comprehensively. Regarding this process, we make the following recommendations.

First, *military intelligence organizations should standardize their MIPE test plans* to facilitate the evaluation of systems that provide MIPE capabilities in general, including both traditional MI-ATR functions and other methods. Metrics and data sets for testing these systems should be developed and standardized. The AFRL COMPASE Center, in collaboration with Air Force Materiel Command (AFMC) and the Air Force ISR Agency (AFISRA), has developed a preliminary list of desired thresholds and objectives for systems that provide MIPE capabilities.[81] It has also created an initial data set as part of its efforts to evaluate the CID module of VIVID. The process undertaken to develop the VIVID data set, as well as the corresponding metrics, can be leveraged to develop a comprehensive truthed data set.[82]

As it is not feasible to completely characterize the efficacy of any MIPE capability for all targets under all conditions, *military intelligence organizations should devise an appropriate truthed data set* to benchmark the effectiveness of MIPE systems, using existing thresholds and

---

[81] Clark, 2009.

[82] Erickson et al., 2007.

objectives to guide this development.[83] The video stream should contain a bank of representative targets relevant to both current operations and anticipated future scenarios. Video sensors expected to be employed in the field should be used to produce the truthed data stream.

Although no data set can encompass every potential scenario, a challenging truthed data set can provide a good basis for informed acquisition. This truthed data set (as well as any other data set used to evaluate MIPE systems performance, truthed or not) should be sequestered from the developer prior to testing. The environmental conditions and sensors employed may be disclosed, but the data set itself should not be released to the developer to ensure that the results of the test are not biased. Military intelligence organizations may consider releasing a small segment of the data set for the purposes of research and development—a segment that should be excluded from the final data set used for the MIPE capability assessment.

Second, military intelligence organizations should use this procedure to examine several competing MIPE systems that provide the same capabilities as part of the initial Phase 1 or developmental evaluation.[84] Several systems or subsystems should be compared against this common test data by taking advantage of an experimentation laboratory and/or Empire Challenge or other exercises.[85] Testing all promising MIPE systems against standard metrics evaluated using the same data set is currently the best way to make an informed decision about acquisition. In the future, military intelligence organizations may also wish to consider holding an open competition involving rival technologies, similar to the DARPA Grand Challenge for robotic vehicles.

Though many attractive features are promised by vendors of MIPE systems, many of these features have not yet been tested or validated. Furthermore, in the open literature, there is little concrete evidence that state-of-the-art technology can fulfill some of the ambitious objectives of certain MIPE systems—namely, those that claim to be able to automatically recognize any object in any environment. Thus, we urge military intelligence organizations to exercise caution in the acquisition of these systems by performing rigorous and detailed testing on the advertised capabilities.

Finally, human-in-the-loop tests are also important. If the human is to be an integral part of the system tested, then the tests need to include the human to replicate real-world conditions. If humans are not included in testing, a system could potentially pass rigorous tests but then fail when it was finally used by humans.

---

[83] A data set that is not rich enough—or is too rich—to test the systems in the range of the desired thresholds will not be useful.

[84] The military intelligence organization may also consider the use of a set of MIPE tools from the outset. The set may comprise complementary tools that can be made to interoperate.

[85] Randy Redman, "Empire Challenge Pulls Worldwide Resources for Exercise," *Air Force Print News Today*, August 24, 2010.

Investment and Acquisition

Despite significant progress in MI-ATR and computer vision research in general, several desirable MIPE capabilities have not yet been achieved. Numerous sophisticated methods for extracting visual information exist today, but they seldom work consistently and robustly in the real, dynamically changing world. Recognition of certain classes of objects, such as human faces, has been achieved with success, but forming recognizable categories or performing recognition when a target is not trivially separable from the image background is only possible in limited scope. Computer vision systems only have a rudimentary ability to recognize activities or actions in the context of their surroundings. Thus, here we make some preliminary recommendations on investment, which do not attempt to be comprehensive. They are, rather, a few examples of what we think should be part of a comprehensive investment strategy for MIPE technologies and systems.

First, military intelligence organizations should make an effort to adopt MIPE technologies and systems that enable the focus-of-attention CONOP. Further, they should adopt the simple CONOP associated with this approach, as described in Chapter Two.

Second, military intelligence organizations should also direct near-term acquisition to focus on MI-ATR technology that enables important niche MIPE capabilities. These capabilities should be identified based both on the maturity of the required MI-ATR function and on the needs of the military organization. As mentioned, the performance of MI-ATR algorithms is heavily dependent on the environment in which they are used; a state-of-the-art MI-ATR system will not be able to recognize an arbitrary object in an arbitrary environment. However, in the near term, MI-ATR systems could perform useful niche tasks, if designed specifically for those tasks. For example, many police cars in the United States are being equipped with roof-mounted cameras to monitor parking sites. These roof-mounted cameras take pictures of license plates and the position of each parked vehicle's tires as the police car drives by. A second pass down the same street will reveal to a police officer which cars have not moved, indicating that those cars should be ticketed.[86] One could imagine a similar change detection task being useful to military forces attempting to characterize vehicular patterns of life in theater. As mentioned previously, to effectively design these niche systems, an appropriate testing and development process would be required.

Third, investment may be targeted to recognition systems that take advantage of many types of information to augment the performance of more-immature methods. This multi-INT approach is well developed, and many products are commercially available. For example, one can take a photo of a restaurant with the Google Android phone and, based on that photo in combination with GPS data and textual clues, receive reviews of the restaurant. Thus, the Android phone uses feature extraction in combination with other types of information to recognize objects in an

---

[86] Jean Guerrero, "Police Cruise for Meter Cheaters Using New Camera Technology," *The Seattle Times*, June 21, 2009.

image. This same multi-INT approach to object recognition could be useful to military analysts if several types of information were automatically synchronized to FMV feeds.

In the near term, military intelligence organizations should procure and invest in MIPE systems based on "low-hanging fruit" technologies.[87] In particular, we recommend MIPE systems that perform background subtraction. These systems will be very useful when exploiting FMV feeds taken on sparse environments, such as those encountered in current operations. A background subtraction algorithm is able to automatically detect whether the foreground of a video feed has changed significantly between frames.[88] An alarm set off by the system can then cue an analyst to focus his or her attention on the changing scene. On the other hand, if the scene is not changing, the analyst may be free to focus on performing a task other than monitoring the video feed. The tool, at least partially, can relieve the analyst from the burden of continuously monitoring a video feed when nothing significant is happening in the feed. The tool may also assist an analyst in exploiting WAMI sensor collections used to explore a relatively unpopulated region. The tool may direct the analyst to focus his or her attention to areas of the feed in which some activity is present. Redirecting a higher resolution sensor to one of those areas of activity may be called for by additional exploitation of the WAMI feed.

Finally, military intelligence organizations should review their acquisition process for MIPE systems and technologies. The diversity of MIPE technologies makes their acquisition—in addition to their evaluation and assessment—challenging. No single end-to-end solution for a panacea, do-it-all MIPE system exists; specific technologies and specific methods facilitate or enable different MIPE functions but may be at differing technology readiness levels. The military intelligence organizations may need to collect the best set of technologies and methods for full system integration or spirally integrate them as they mature. However, it is difficult to assess the interoperability of hundreds of combinations of subsystems. Furthermore, it may be difficult to spirally integrate or upgrade technologies and methods in the military because of stringent requirements on modifications to a weapons system.

It is DoD's practice to place one organization in charge of development and another in charge of sustainment. However, what works well with a long-term acquisition program, such as a fighter or bomber, may not be well suited for acquiring MIPE systems, as the technology evolves very quickly. It may be advantageous to have a single entity coordinating the diverse organizations and projects related to MIPE so as to be able to "catch up" with the rapidly evolving commercial sector, for example. Even if such a broad approach to MIPE systems is not adopted, a single entity should advise the respective program offices on managing the MIPE evaluation process, including research, testing, and acquisition. This entity should also serve as a

---

[87] That is, technologies that are already mature and are relatively easy to implement.

[88] A significant change in the video scene could be defined as simply a significant change in the average value of pixels in the foreground between two video frames. This value could be determined via testing or specified by an analyst in real time.

clearinghouse for MIPE technologies, as well as a "smart buyer" advisor. Ideally, this lead MIPE evaluation entity would have extensive knowledge of MIPE technology and current systems in development, as well as the specific needs of military intelligence organizations.

Conclusion

MIPE capabilities have the potential to help imagery intelligence analysts cope with, and make best use of, the massive amounts of data being collected around the world. Although much of the enabling technology is still in development, there are near-term steps that military intelligence organizations can take to test, evaluate, and select MIPE systems and capabilities that meet current needs. Strategic investments and acquisition practices, such as those described in this report, can help MIPE technologies continue to keep pace with the ever-growing demand for motion imagery analysis.

Appendix: Summary of Video Analytics Technology from Pacific Northwest National Laboratory

Two papers by Harold Trease and colleagues at Pacific Northwest National Laboratory (PNNL) published in the proceedings of a conference held by the International Association of Science and Technology Development present a system designed to create searchable index tables that can be used to access large quantities of video without textual or audio metadata tags.[89, 90] These algorithms promise to organize objects, or "entities," in a video stream into a searchable database by automatically defining an "entity index table" and "table of contents." PNNL refers to this methodology as *video analytics*. We present here a summary of these two papers. This appendix is provided for the savvy technical reader as an example of MIPE technology[91] for which a description of important features can be found in the public domain.[92]

Populating an Entity Index Table or "Glossary"

Video analytic algorithms identify subsections, or entities, in a video sequence on a frame-by-frame basis. In each frame, measurements of information (color and pixel distribution) are taken for each subsection of a frame, down to some specified pixel size. Specifically, five measurements of the distribution of each of four colors (red, blue, green, and gray) are used to characterize each entity of each frame, as shown in Figure A.1. The information associated with each entity is then stored as a string of 20 numbers in an organized, indexed database. These 20-dimensional "signatures" may be approximated in three dimensions using principal component analysis (PCA) and plotted, as shown in Figure A.2.[93] If two objects have strings of numbers that are within a defined tolerance, they are deemed the same object.

---

[89] Trease et al, 2008.

[90] Trease and Trease, 2009.

[91] Video analytics also has some MIDS capabilities.

[92] Detailed information on existing MIPE technologies and systems tends to be proprietary.

[93] Via experimentation, PNNL has shown that a three-element signature contains 98–99 percent of the information contained in the 20-element signature of a video frame.

Figure A.1. Five Measurements of the Distribution of Four Colors Are Used to Characterize Each Frame or Subframe in a Video Sequence

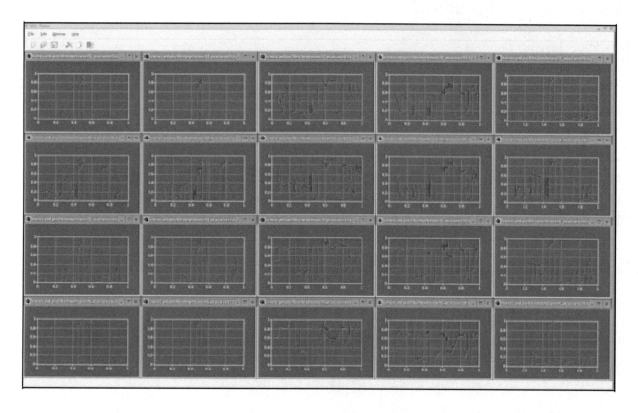

SOURCE: Trease and Trease, 2009.

Figure A.2. Using Principle Component Analysis to Approximate a 20-Component Frame Signature in Three Components, Each Frame May Be Mapped in Three-Dimensional Space

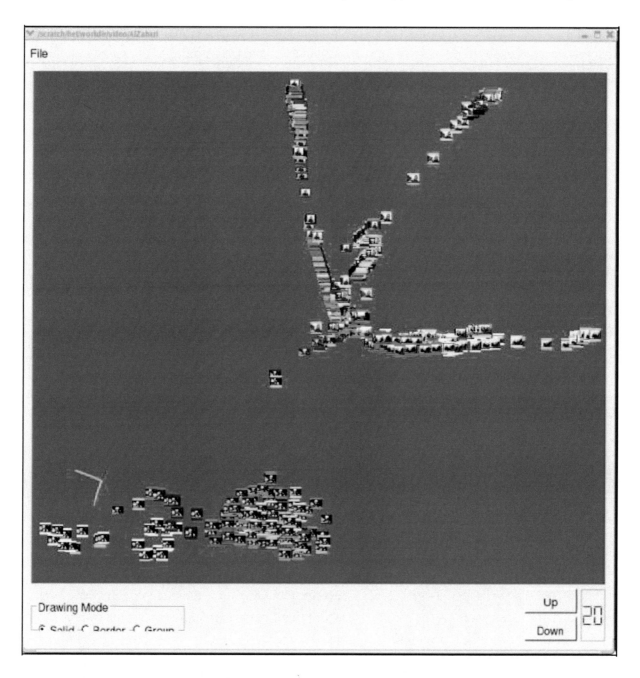

SOURCE: Trease and Trease, 2009.

All entities contained in a video sequence are then cataloged by the PNNL algorithm into an entity index table. The entity index table works much like a glossary, listing all frames that contain a specified entity of interest.

Developing a Table of Contents

The PNNL algorithm also populates a table of contents (associated with a video segment) by identifying a large overall change between two concurrent frames. As mentioned, a 20-element signature defines each frame in a video; a large change in the magnitude, or average value, of this signature indicates an overall change in the content of the video, as shown in Figure A.3. Thus, a video segment may be divided into sections of similar content by noting where overall changes in the 20-element signature occur.

Figure A.3. Overall Changes in Video Content Are Indicated in the Table of Contents

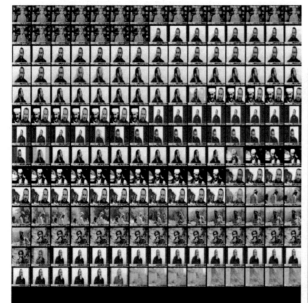 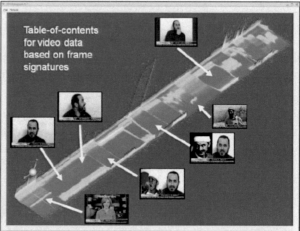

SOURCE: Trease and Trease, 2009.

System-Level Framework for Video Analytics

The workflow process of a video analytics system includes four main steps. First, raw data from streaming video cameras (or a database of archived video) are entered into the system. Next, algorithms, described previously for table of contents and entity index table generation, are employed. Then the analysis of unique signatures combined with PCA reduces the quantity of video data while preserving important dimensions. The final step is the generation and analysis of graphs to provide a basis for face and object recognition, ad hoc "video-based social network" construction and analysis, and the recognition of behavioral patterns based on the time and space relationships across video streams.

To accomplish this final step, graph theory is employed to populate and analyze the ad hoc video-based social network. Using video analytic methods, a signature (either 20-dimensional or three-dimensional) represents each object, including each person or face in a video. Thus, the proximity of two objects may be defined as the minimum distance between the two objects' signatures. Through examination of the proximity of different objects' signatures, network analysis methods may be employed to quantify the degree to which these objects are connected. Since each point in the graph represents a frame of video (or a face or object), this connectedness facilitates analysis of video-based social interactions. These types of interactions may indicate if a person has been seen before, a person's close associates, and distinguishing patterns of behavior.

A computer network to support system-level functionality of a video analytics system must include the following:

1. networked multicore processors with high-speed connections (these may be separated over large distances)
2. network control of timing and workflow of major processes of the system
3. management of data flow (raw and processed video) throughout the system
4. a communication network to manage messages passed between master and slave nodes in the network.

As of the time of the publication in the International Association of Science and Technology Development conference proceedings, components of the network included a Linux cluster, an IBM BE Cell (PS3) cluster, an Nvidia GPGPU cluster, and a Cray XMT.

References

"All Too Much: Monstrous Amounts of Data," *The Economist*, February 25, 2010. As of November 17, 2012
http://www.economist.com/node/15557421

Antani, Sameer, Rangachar Kasturi, and Ramesh Jain, "A Survey on the Use of Pattern Recognition Methods for Abstraction, Indexing, and Retrieval of Images and Video," *Journal of Pattern Recognition*, Vol. 35, 2002, pp. 945–965.

Aristidou, A., P. Pangalos, and H. Aghvami, "Tracking Multiple Sports Players for Mobile Display," IPCV Conference, 2007. As of July 26, 2011:
http://http://www.andreasaristidou.com/publications/Tracking_IPCV_2007.pdf

Axis Communications, "H.264 Video Compression Standard—New Possibilities Within Video Surveillance," 2008. As of July 19, 2011:
http://www.wavestore.com/download.php?white_paper=2

Benezeth, Y., P. M. Jodoin, B. Emile, H. Laurent, and C. Rosenberger, "Review and Evaluation of Commonly-Implemented Background Subtraction Algorithms," 19th International Conference on Pattern Recognition, 2008.

Chaisorn, L., C. Manders, and S. Rahardja, "Video Retrieval—Evolution of Video Segmentation, Indexing and Search," in *2nd IEEE International Conference on Computer Science and Information Technology (ICCSIT)*, August 8–11, 2009, pp. 16–20.

Clark, Lloyd G., AFRL/RYAA, "AFRL COMPASE Center," PowerPoint presentation, December 17, 2009.

Cordova, Amado, Kirsten M. Keller, Lance Menthe, and Carl Rhodes, *Virtual Collaboration for a Distributed Enterprise,* Santa Monica, Calif.: RAND Corporation, RR-153-AF, 2013. As of October 15, 2013:
http://www.rand.org/pubs/research_reports/RR153.html

Cordova, Amado, Lance Menthe, Lindsay D. Millard, Kirsten M. Keller, Carl Rhodes, and Jeffrey Sullivan, *Emerging Technologies for Intelligence Analysts: Recommendations for the Air Force DCGS Enterprise*, Santa Monica, Calif.: RAND Corporation, 2012, not available to the general public.

D'Agostino, Davi M., Director, Defense Capabilities and Management, Intelligence, Surveillance, and Reconnaissance, "Overarching Guidance Is Needed to Advance Information Sharing," testimony before the Subcommittees on Air and Land Forces and Seapower and Expeditionary Forces, Committee on Armed Services, House of

Representatives, Washington, D.C.: U.S. Government Accountability Office, GAO-10-500T, March 17, 2010. As of February 8, 2011:
http://www.gao.gov/new.items/d10500t.pdf

DARPA Information Innovation Office, "Video and Image Retrieval and Analysis Tool (VIRAT)," undated. As of January 5, 2012:
http://www.darpa.mil/Our_Work/I2O/Programs/Video_and_Image_Retrieval_and_Analysis_Tool_(VIRAT).asp

"Data, Data Everywhere," *The Economist*, February 25, 2010. As of November 17, 2012:
http://www.economist.com/node/15557443

Defense Procurement and Acquisition Policy Office of the Under Secretary of Defense (Acquisition, Technology and Logistics), *Manager's Guide to Technology Transition in an Evolutionary Acquisition Environment*, version 1.0, January 31, 2003.

Delay, John, "Mastering Motion Imagery," *C4ISR Journal*, November/December 2009, pp. 42–44.

Department of Defense, *Close Air Support*, Joint Publication 3-09.3, July 8, 2009.

———, *Quadrennial Defense Review Report*, February 2010.

———, *DoD Dictionary of Military and Associated Terms*, Joint Publication 1-02, as amended through April 2010.

Department of Defense/Intelligence Community/National System for Geospatial Intelligence (DoD/IC/NSG) Motion Imagery Standards Board (MISB), *Motion Imagery Standards Profile Version 5.4*, December 3, 2009.

Deptula, David A., keynote speech, C4ISR Journal Conference, Arlington, Va., October 2009.

———, "Air Force ISR in a Changing World," *Proceedings of the Royal Australian Air Force Air Power Conference*, Canberra, Australia, March 30, 2010.

Deptula, David A., and James R. Marrs, "Global Distributed ISR Operations: The Changing Face of Warfare," *Joint Force Quarterly*, Issue 54, July 2009, pp. 110–115. As of September 10, 2010:
http://www.ndu.edu/press/lib/images/jfq-54/26.pdf

Deputy Under Secretary of Defense (Advanced Systems & Concepts), *JCTD Practical Operating Guidelines (POG) Narrative Description*, version 2.0, March 2009, p. 1.

DoD/IC/NSG MISB—*see* Department of Defense/Intelligence Community/National System for Geospatial Intelligence (DoD/IC/NSG) Motion Imagery Standards Board (MISB).

Drew, Christopher, "Drones Are Weapons of Choice in Fighting Qaeda," *New York Times*, March 16, 2009.

————, "The Military Is Awash in Data from Drones," *New York Times*, January 11, 2010.

Eklundh, Jan-Olof, and Henrik I. Christensen, "Computer Vision: Past and Future," in Reinhard Wilhelm, ed., *Informatics: 10 Years Back, 10 Years Ahead (Lecture Notes in Computer Science)*, Springer, 2001, pp. 328–340.

Erickson, Kyle J., Philip M. Hanna, Lori A. Westerkamp, and John C. Mossing, "Evaluation of the VIVID Confirmatory Identification Module," in *Automatic Target Recognition XVII, Proceedings of SPIE*, Vol. 6566, 6566B, 2007.

Gentile, Keith E., *The Future of Airborne Reconnaissance*, Quantico, Va.: Marine Corps Command and Staff College, March 27, 1996.

Geospatial Intelligence Standards Working Group (GWG), *Charter*, revised 2009. As of July 1, 2011:
http://www.gwg.nga.mil/documents/GWG_Charter.pdf

Gerber, Cheryl, "Full Speed Ahead for Full Motion Video," *Geospatial Intelligence Forum*, Vol. 7, No. 5, October 2009, pp. 36–40.

Guerrero, Jean, "Police Cruise for Meter Cheaters Using New Camera Technology," *The Seattle Times*, June 21, 2009. As of February 8, 2011:
http://seattletimes.nwsource.com/html/localnews/2009364600_parkingstory21.html

Gupte, Surendra, Osama Masoud, Robert R. K. Martin, and Nikolaos P. Papanikolopoulos, "Detection and Classification of Vehicles," *IEEE Transactions on Intelligent Transportation Systems*, Vol. 3, No. 1, March 2002.

Hodson, Steven, "Skype Commands 13 Percent of International Phone Calls," *The Inquisitr*, May 3, 2010. As of February 8, 2011:
http://www.inquisitr.com/71802/skype-commands-13-percent-of-international-calls/

Iannotta, Ben, "Playing Catch-Up," *C4ISR Journal*, October 2009, pp. 26–28.

————, "Fallen Angel," *C4ISR Journal*, July 1, 2010. As of August 2, 2010:
http://www.c4isrjournal.com/story.php?F=4661989

Institute for Telecommunications Sciences, "Kalman Filter," August 23, 1996. As of November 14, 2011:
http://www.its.bldrdoc.gov/fs-1037/dir-020/_2930.htm

Irvine, John M., "Assessing Target Search Performance: The Free-Response Operator Characteristic Model," *Optical Engineering*, Vol. 43, No. 12, December 2004.

Isaacs, Ellen A., and John C. Tang, "What Video Can and Can't Do for Collaboration: A Case Study," *Multimedia Systems*, Vol. 2, 1994, pp. 63–73.

Jamieson, VeraLinn, untitled entry, *C4ISR Journal*, October 1, 2009.

Kahn, Scott D., "On the Future of Genomic Data," *Science*, Vol. 331, February 2011, p. 11. As of November 17, 2012:
http://www.sciencemag.org/content/331/6018/728.full

Lakhani, Karim R., "Google Wave's Decision," *Harvard Business Review*, August 6, 2010.

Levine, Martin D., "Feature Extraction: A Survey," *Proceedings of the IEEE*, Vol. 57, No. 8, August 1969.

Magnuson, Stew, "Military 'Swimming in Sensors and Drowning in Data,'" *National Defense Magazine*, January 2010. As of September 3, 2010:
http://www.nationaldefensemagazine.org/archive/2010/January/Pages/Military%E2%80%98 SwimmingInSensorsandDrowninginData%E2%80%99.aspx

Matthews, William, "One Sensor to Do the Work of Many: BAE, DARPA Lash Up Hundreds of 5-Megapixel Camera Chips," *Defense News*, March 1, 2010.

Menthe, Lance, Amado Cordova, Carl Rhodes, Rachel Costello, and Jeffrey Sullivan, *The Future of Air Force Motion Imagery Exploitation: Lessons from the Commercial World,* Santa Monica, Calif.: RAND Corporation, TR-1133-AF, 2012. As of October 15, 2013:
http://www.rand.org/pubs/technical_reports/TR1133.html

Murphy, Robin R., and Brent Taylor, "A Survey of Machine Learning Techniques for Automatic Target Recognition," *IEEE Transactions on Pattern Analysis and Machine Intelligence*, Golden, Colo.: Department of Mathematical and Computer Sciences, Colorado School of Mines, 2007.

National Geospatial-Intelligence Agency, "Geospatial Intelligence (GEOINT) Basic Doctrine," Publication 1-0, September 2006. As of June 28, 2011:
http://www.fas.org/irp/agency/nga/doctrine.pdf

———, *National Center for Geospatial Intelligence Standards*, undated. As of July 1, 2011:
https://www1.nga.mil/ProductsServices/geointstandards/Documents/Brochures/NCGISbroch ure.pdf

Office of the Secretary of Defense, *The Integrated Airborne Reconnaissance Architecture, Executive Summary*, Washington, D.C.: Defense Airborne Reconnaissance Office, 1994.

———, *1996 Annual Defense Report*, Washington, D.C., 1996.

Pagels, Michael A., "Heterogeneous Airborne Reconnaissance Team," DARPA, August 2008.

Photosynth home page, undated. As of December 12, 2011:
http://photosynth.net/

Piccardi, Massimo, "Background Subtraction Techniques: A Review," *IEEE International Conference on Systems, Man and Cybernetics*, 2004. As of July 25, 2011: http://profs.sci.univr.it/~cristanm/teaching/sar_files/lezione4/Piccardi.pdf

Redman, Randy, "Empire Challenge Pulls Worldwide Resources for Exercise," *Air Force Print News Today*, August 24, 2010. As of December 1, 2011: http://www.af.mil/news/story_print.asp?id=123218969

Richfield, Paul, "New Video System Takes on Wide-Area Sensor Challenge," *Defense System Magazine*, April 6, 2011. As of June 29, 2011: http://defensesystems.com/articles/2011/03/29/c4isr-1-battlefield-full-motion-video.aspx

Schanz, M. V., "The Reaper Harvest," *Air Force Magazine*, April 2011. As of June 28, 2011: http://www.airforce-magazine.com/MagazineArchive/Pages/2011/April%202011/0411reaper.aspx

Siegel, Anna, "Warfighters Reach Back to Langley," *Air Combat Command Public Affairs*, October 8, 2003.

Siemens, "Telscan," September 24, 2010. As of July 26, 2011: http://www.siemens.co.uk/traffic/en/index/productssolutionsservices/faultandmonitoring/telscan.htm

Smith, Paul L., *Transforming Air Force Intelligence*, Maxwell AFB, Ga.: Air War College, February 14, 2007.

Szeliski, Richard, *Computer Vision: Algorithms and Applications*, New York: Springer, 2010.

Tirpak, John A., "Beyond Reachback," *Air Force Magazine*, March 2009.

Toderici, George, Hrishikesh Aradhye, Marius Pasca, Luciano Sbaiz, and Jay Yagnik, "Finding Meaning on YouTube: Tag Recommendation and Category Discovery," in *2010 IEEE Conference on Computer Vision and Pattern Recognition (CVPR)*, June 13–18, 2010, pp. 3447–3454.

Trease, Harold, Robert Farber, Adam Wynne, and Lynne Trease, "High Performance Video Content Analysis Using Hybrid, Multi-Core Processors," in *Proceedings of the 10th IASTED International Conference*, Signal and Image Processing, Kailua-Kona, Hawaii, August 18–20, 2008.

Trease, Harold, and Lynn Trease, "Video Analytics for Indexing, Summarization, and Searching of Video Archives," in *Proceedings of the IASTED International Conference, Signal and Image Processing*, Honolulu, Hawaii, August 17–19, 2009.

Trucco, Emanuele, and Konstantinos Plakas, "Video Tracking: A Concise Survey," *IEEE Journal of Oceanic Engineering*, Vol. 31, No. 2, April 2006.

Turaga, Pavan, Rama Chellapa, V. S. Subrahmanian, and Octavian Udrea, "Machine Recognition of Human Activities: A Survey," *IEEE Transactions on Circuits and Systems for Video Technology*, Vol. 18, No. 11, November 2008.

U.S. Air Force, "The Vision and Strategy for United States Air Force Intelligence, Surveillance and Reconnaissance," Washington, D.C.: Headquarters United States Air Force, July 19, 2010.

U.S. Government Accountability Office, *Unmanned Aircraft Systems: New DOD Programs Can Learn from Past Efforts to Craft Better and Less Risky Acquisition Strategies*, Washington, D.C., GAO-06-447, March 2006. As of February 8, 2011: http://www.gao.gov/new.items/d06447.pdf

Yang, Yan, B. C. Lovell, and F. Dadgostar, "Content-Based Video Retrieval (CBVR) System for CCTV Surveillance Videos," in *Digital Image Computing: Techniques and Applications 2009*, December 1–3, 2009, pp. 183–187.

Young, John J., Under Secretary of Defense for Acquisition, Technology and Logistics, "Hearing Before the Committee on Armed Services," U.S. Senate, June 3, 2008.

Zhao, W., R. Chellappa, P. J. Phillips, and A. Rosenfeld, "Face Recognition: A Literature Survey," *ACM Computing Surveys*, Vol. 35, No. 4, December 2008, pp. 399–458.